BELVEDERE ELEMENTARY SCHOOL
READING PROGRAM

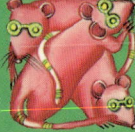

Who Knows?

Some nursery rhymes are just nonsense rhymes that sound fun when you say them. But many nursery rhymes do, in fact, have a story to tell. Sometimes the story is as extraordinary as the rhyme itself.

Rigby
ISBN: 0-7901-1836-X

CONTENTS

History and Mystery	2
Old Nursery Rhymes	4
Rain, Rain, Go Away	4
I'm the King of the Castle	6
Thirty Days Hath September	8
Old King Cole	10
Jack and Jill Went Up the Hill	12
Oranges and Lemons	14
Ring-a-ring o' Roses	16
Sing a Song of Sixpence	18
Real Nursery Folk	20
Humpty Dumpty	20
Little Jack Horner	22
Doctor Foster	24
The Grand Old Duke of York	26
Mary, Mary, Quite Contrary	28
Little Miss Muffet	30
Mary Had a Little Lamb	32
Explanation, Please!	34
Seesaw, Margery Daw	34
Hot Cross Buns	36
Jack Be Nimble	38
Ladybug, Ladybug	40
Rock-a-bye, Baby	42
The Most Sung Song	44
Happy Birthday	44
Index of First Lines	46

HISTORY AND MYSTERY

Throughout history, people have recited rhymes and sung songs for their children. When the children grew up, they taught *their* children the same rhymes and songs.

Some nursery rhymes have been kept alive like this for hundreds, even thousands, of years. Often these rhymes weren't even written down. People just remembered them and passed them on by word of mouth.

Who were the mysterious authors of these rhymes? When did these authors live? Why did they write these rhymes, and why did they keep their identities secret? Behind these well-known rhymes, there are many interesting stories.

SOME NURSERY RHYME DATES

500 B.C.
Rain, Rain, Go Away

A.D. **1500**
Three Blind Mice

A.D. **100**
Thirty Days Hath September

A.D. **1550**
Ding Dong Bell, Pussy's in the Well

A.D. **300**
Old King Cole

A.D. **1600**
Sing a Song of Sixpence

A.D. **1200**
Jack and Jill Went Up the Hill

A.D. **1700**
Hey Diddle Diddle

A.D. **1300**
Baa, Baa, Black Sheep

A.D. **1800**
Polly Put the Kettle On

OLD NURSERY RHYMES

RAIN, RAIN, GO AWAY

*Rain, rain, go away,
Come again another day.*

This is one of the oldest nursery rhymes in the world. Parents in ancient Greece and Rome used to ask their children to chant this rhyme as a magic charm to make the rain stop. In those days, people believed that only children had the power to change the weather.

It may not always have stopped the rain, but people must have enjoyed the rhyme, because two and a half thousand years later, children are still chanting it!

I'M THE KING OF THE CASTLE

*I'm the king of the castle
And you're the dirty rascal.*

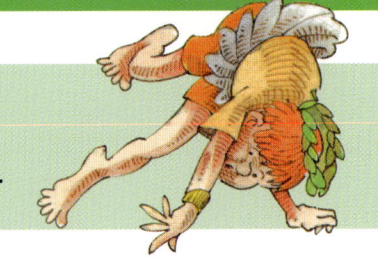

This little rhyme comes from Roman times, too. Horace, a famous poet, quoted it in the year 20 B.C.

You may have played a game of King of the Castle (or King of the Hill). One person stands on top of a mound or a raised object and declares that he or she is the king or queen of the castle. The others then try to push the person off the mound to become the new king or queen. Two thousand years ago, Roman children would make a mound of sand and play this very same game.

THIRTY DAYS HATH SEPTEMBER

*Thirty days hath September,
April, June, and November;
All the rest have thirty-one,
Excepting February alone,
And that has twenty-eight days clear
And twenty-nine in each leap year.*

The first record we have of this rhyme being written down comes from the thirteenth century, when a French writer put it on paper. But versions of it probably go back to Roman times.

In fact, we owe the basis of our modern calendar to one of the most famous Roman rulers, Julius Caesar. He decided that a calendar should have four months of thirty days and seven months of thirty-one days. One month, February, has twenty-eight days in ordinary years and twenty-nine every fourth, or leap, year.

OLD KING COLE

Old King Cole was a merry old soul,
And a merry old soul was he;
He called for his pipe,
And he called for his bowl,
And he called for his fiddlers three.

Every fiddler, he had a fine fiddle,
And a very fine fiddle had he;
Twee tweedle dee, tweedle dee, went the fiddlers.
Oh, there's none so rare as can compare
With King Cole and his fiddlers three.

In the third century, a duke by the name of Coel is said to have built the city of Colchester in Britain. Later, he became King Coel. His daughter, Helen, was a fine musician, which might explain the king's devotion to his "fiddlers three" in the rhyme.

JACK AND JILL WENT UP THE HILL

*Jack and Jill went up the hill
To fetch a pail of water;
Jack fell down and broke his crown,
And Jill came tumbling after.*

*Up Jack got and home did trot,
As fast as he could caper,
To Old Dame Dob, who patched his nob
With vinegar and brown paper.*

It is possible this rhyme may have come from the Norse raiders of Scandinavia, who invaded the British Isles in the twelfth and thirteenth centuries.

In Scandinavian mythology, there is a legend about two children, Hjuki and Bil, who went to a well for water, carrying a bucket suspended from a pole. Hjuki in Norse would have been pronounced "Juki," which could easily have become "Jack." "Bil" could have become "Jill."

In the story, as the two children were returning from the well, Mani the moon scooped them up and carried them off. So now, according to the legend, when you look up at the full moon, you can see the shadowy shapes of the two trapped children carrying their bucket of water.

ORANGES AND LEMONS

*Oranges and lemons,
Say the bells of St. Clement's.*

*You owe me ten shillings,
Say the bells of St. Helen's.*

*When will you pay me?
Say the bells of Old Bailey.*

*When I grow rich,
Say the bells of Shoreditch.*

*Pray when will that be?
Say the bells of Stepney.*

*I'm sure I don't know,
Says the great bell at Bow.*

*Here comes the candle
   to light you to bed,
And here comes a chopper
   to chop off your head.
(Chop! Chop! Chop! Chop!
   Last man's head!)*

One theory about this rhyme is that it is really about two of King Henry VIII's wives, Anne Boleyn and Catherine Howard, who were beheaded in London.

This gruesome story became a popular children's game. Two people (an orange and a lemon) link hands to form an arch. The others parade in a circle, passing under the arms as they recite the rhyme. When it comes to the last line, the person passing under the arch is caught. (Everyone shouts, "Chop! Chop! Chop!...") The victim is asked if he or she would like to be a lemon or an orange, then joins a line behind the "orange" or the "lemon" person. The game ends with a tug-of-war.

RING-A-RING O' ROSES

*Ring-a-ring o' roses,
A pocket full of posies,
A-tishoo! A-tishoo!
We all fall down.*

For centuries, children have held hands in a ring and had fun chanting these words while playing out the actions.

On the surface, the words sound very charming. Yet the rhyme probably goes back to the seventeenth century when Britain was in the grim grip of the Great Plague. One of the signs of this dreaded disease was a red circle, or "ring o' roses," on the skin.

People used to carry little bundles of special herbs and dried flowers that they hoped would keep the plague away.

In the rhyme, this is a "pocket full of posies." Elder leaves, cinnamon, rue, nutmeg, cloves, and onions were thought to help give protection from the plague.

Sneezing – "A-tishoo! A-tishoo!" – was one of the signs that you had the disease. People with the plague often became ill so quickly that they would fall down in the street – hence the last line.

SING A SONG OF SIXPENCE

Sing a song of sixpence,
A pocket full of rye;
Four and twenty blackbirds
Baked in a pie.

When the pie was opened,
The birds began to sing;
Wasn't that a dainty dish
To set before the king?

The king was in his counting-house,
Counting out his money;
The queen was in the parlor,
Eating bread and honey.

The maid was in the garden,
Hanging out the clothes;
Along came a blackbird
And nipped off her nose.

In 1598, an Italian recipe book was translated into English. It proved to be very popular. One of the recipes told how to make a pie with live birds inside so that when the crust was cut, the birds would fly out and surprise the guests.

This became a popular entertainment. The startled birds would fly out of the pie, giving everyone a fright. It's not something that we would do today!

REAL NURSERY FOLK

HUMPTY DUMPTY

*Humpty Dumpty sat on a wall.
Humpty Dumpty had a great fall.
All the king's horses and all the king's men
Couldn't put Humpty together again.*

Years ago, if you were caught criticizing your king or ruling lord, you were likely to be thrown in jail. Worse, you might even have your head chopped off!

One way around this problem was to write what seemed to be a harmless little rhyme for children, which was, in fact, a poem making fun of someone important, or criticizing something the king or the government had done.

"Humpty Dumpty" may have been a poem making fun of King Charles I. As the rhyme says, when he fell from favor, despite all his troops and horse soldiers, no one could save him.

LITTLE JACK HORNER

*Little Jack Horner
Sat in the corner,
Eating his Christmas pie;
He put in his thumb
And pulled out a plum,
And said, "What a good boy am I!"*

According to popular legend, "little Jack Horner" was, in fact, Thomas Horner, who worked for the Abbot of Glastonbury, England. The abbot had a surprise Christmas pie made for the king. Inside the pie were hidden the title deeds to twelve manors. He entrusted this special gift to Thomas Horner and sent him to give it to the king.

But, on the way, Horner peeped under the crust. According to legend, he found the title deeds and decided to keep the best one – a "plum" – for himself.

DOCTOR FOSTER

*Doctor Foster went to Gloucester
In a shower of rain;
He stepped in a puddle
Right up to his middle,
And never went there again.*

Who was Doctor Foster? According to popular belief, he was really King Edward I, who once came to visit the city of Gloucester, England. He arrived on a very rainy day and, as he was riding up the main street, his horse floundered in the mud and became completely stuck.

This was a most undignified thing to happen to a king. Ropes and wood planks were quickly brought and, with the help of many men, the king and his horse were finally pulled from the mud. The king was so furious that he vowed he would never visit Gloucester again.

By the way, the words "puddle" and "middle" do not rhyme very well. Originally, the rhyme may have used the old form of the word *puddle*, pronounced and spelled *piddle*.

THE GRAND OLD DUKE OF YORK

*Oh, the grand old Duke of York,
He had ten thousand men;
He marched them up to the top of a hill,
And he marched them down again!*

*And when they were up, they were up,
And when they were down, they were down,
And when they were only halfway up,
They were neither up nor down.*

In 1794, the Duke of York was made Commander in Chief of the English army in the Netherlands. As winter began, he found himself with ten thousand soldiers who hadn't been provided with suitable winter clothing.

In those days, when winter set in, armies usually waited for warmer weather before they started fighting. But the French decided otherwise. They went along the frozen canals and surprised the English.

Back in England, there was a great public outcry. Everyone blamed the Duke of York. Someone penned this rhyme, and soon everyone was singing it as a joke.

There is no evidence that the Duke ever marched up and down a hill. In fact, in the Netherlands, where the fighting took place, the land is quite flat. But someone had to be blamed for losing the war.

MARY, MARY, QUITE CONTRARY

Mary, Mary, quite contrary,
How does your garden grow?
With silver bells and cockle shells,
And pretty maids all in a row.

This rhyme is thought to be about Mary, Queen of Scots. Though born in Scotland, she spent most of her childhood in France, where eventually she married the dauphin, the heir to the French throne. Two years later, he died and she returned to Scotland.

But Mary, Queen of Scots, was never very popular in her homeland. The Scots were shocked by her French lifestyle. They thought of her as "contrary."

Mary liked to dress well. One of her favorite gowns was given to her by her French husband, the dauphin.

It was elaborately decorated with, among other things, "silver bells and cockle shells." The "pretty maids all in a row" were probably her four ladies-in-waiting, all of whom were also named Mary!

LITTLE MISS MUFFET

*Little Miss Muffet
Sat on a tuffet,
Eating her curds and whey;
There came a big spider,
Who sat down beside her
And frightened Miss Muffet away.*

It is thought that Miss Muffet was a little girl named Patience Muffet, born at the end of the sixteenth century. Her father was Dr. Thomas Muffet, a famous entomologist (a person who studies insects). Patience grew up surrounded by her father's creepy-crawly pets, which also included spiders.

We don't know for certain that Patience was frightened of spiders. This rhyme was really a joke aimed at making fun of her father. The "tuffet" was probably a grassy mound or hill, although it could have been a three-legged stool.

MARY HAD A LITTLE LAMB

*Mary had a little lamb,
Its fleece was white as snow;
And everywhere that Mary went,
The lamb was sure to go.*

*It followed her to school one day,
That was against the rule;
It made the children laugh and play
To see a lamb at school.*

There is quite a dispute over who "Mary" was. Sarah Hale lived in Boston and edited a magazine that published poems for children. In 1830, she published this poem, which she said was based on "partly true" events. Because she put her initials under the poem, it was assumed that she had written it.

Then Mary Tyler claimed that the poem had been written by John Roulston, and she had been the original Mary.

People were so impressed with Mary Tyler's claim that the local schoolhouse was restored as a memorial.

From Wales came a claim that Mary Hughes had been Sarah Hale's original Mary. Unfortunately, Mary Hughes' lamb followed her to school in 1847, and the poem was published in 1830. So we are still none the wiser!

EXPLANATION, PLEASE!

SEESAW, MARGERY DAW

Seesaw, Margery Daw,
Jacky shall have a new master;
Jacky must have but a penny a day,
Because he can't work any faster.

This rhyme is often sung by children playing on a seesaw. However, the seesaw chant didn't appear until about 1700, while the rhyme is from an earlier time.

"Seesaw, Margery Daw" probably began as a chant recited by sawyers sawing planks of timber. The men, pushing and pulling on a two-man saw, would often use a rhyme like this to set up a rhythm to work to. This explains why Jacky is paid only one penny each day, "because he can't work any faster."

HOT CROSS BUNS

*Hot cross buns, hot cross buns!
One a penny, two a penny,
Hot cross buns!
If you have no daughters,
Give them to your sons;
One a penny, two a penny,
Hot cross buns!*

In the seventeenth and eighteenth centuries, you would have heard this rhyme called out in the street as vendors of hot cross buns went about selling their wares.

Hot cross buns, however, are much older than the rhyme. They date back to pagan times. For many years, spiced cakes were made with a cross on them to keep evil spirits away. Even today, some people still follow the annual custom of hanging a hot cross bun in the kitchen.

They believe it protects the people in the house from evil and brings everyone good luck.

JACK BE NIMBLE

*Jack be nimble, Jack be quick,
Jack jump over the candlestick.*

For many centuries, a popular game was to tell your future by jumping over a lit candle. If the candle stayed alight, then you would have good luck in the days ahead. If the candle went out, ill fortune was just around the corner.

The game was particularly enjoyed by lacemakers. The patron saint of lacemakers was St. Catherine of Alexandria, and St. Catherine's Day, falling on November 25, was always a great holiday for lacemakers.

They celebrated it with special cakes and a drink they called "hot pot." In the evening, they would gather in circles around a lit candle and try their fortune playing "Jack Be Nimble."

LADYBUG, LADYBUG

*Ladybug, ladybug, fly away home,
Your house is on fire and your children all gone;
All except one, and that's little Ann,
And she has crept under the warming pan.*

There are many stories about ladybugs. Through the centuries, ladybugs have been linked with magic and thought to bring good fortune. The stories can be traced back to ancient Egypt and Isis, the Egyptian goddess of magic. There is a very old custom of placing a ladybug on your finger, reciting the rhyme, and blowing once on the ladybug. When the ladybug flies "away home," it is thought to bring good luck.

Other names for ladybugs include lady beetle, ladybird, Marigold, and a name from Norfolk – Bishy Bishy Barnaby!

ROCK-A-BYE, BABY

*Rock-a-bye, baby, on the treetop;
When the wind blows, the cradle will rock;
When the bough breaks, the cradle will fall;
Down will come baby, cradle and all.*

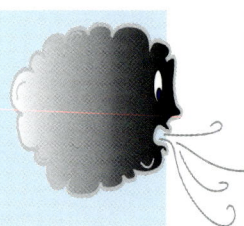

This is one of the oldest known cradle songs. Every night, many babies are sung to sleep with these terrifying words. It's just as well babies don't know what the words mean, for the thought of falling down from treetops would hardly be something to make them sleep!

However, the origin of this song isn't too terrifying. It refers to an ancient custom of hanging babies from branches in baskets made of rushes. As the tree swayed in the wind, the cradle rocked from a bough. Lulled by the movement and the soothing voice of the singer, the baby would go to sleep.

THE MOST SUNG SONG

HAPPY BIRTHDAY

*Happy birthday to you,
Happy birthday to you,
Happy birthday, dear...,
Happy birthday to you.*

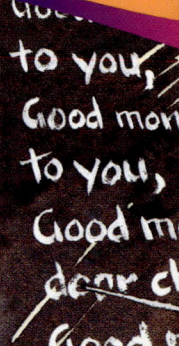

Patty Hill was an enthusiastic teacher who believed school should be cheerful. With her sister, Mildred, a music teacher, she took over duties at a school in Louisville, Kentucky, in the 1890s.

To start the day in a cheerful way, they made up a song with the words:

*Good morning to you,
Good morning to you,
Good morning, dear children,
Good morning to you.*

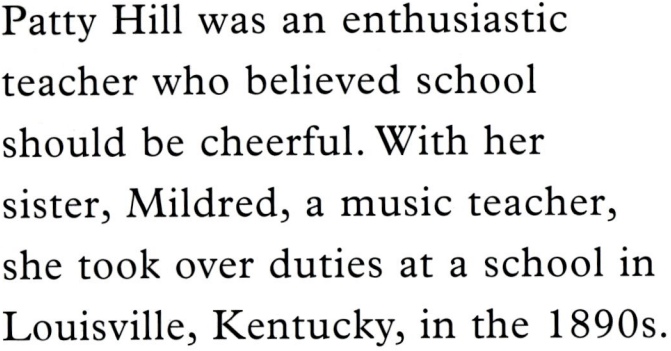

Knowing that most people like to share their birthdays, the teachers later rewrote the words so that the song became "Happy Birthday."

This version of the song spread to other schools and other countries. Today, it is probably the best-known song in the world.

INDEX OF FIRST LINES

Doctor Foster went to Gloucester	24
Happy birthday to you	44
Hot cross buns, hot cross buns	36
Humpty Dumpty sat on a wall	20
I'm the king of the castle	6
Jack and Jill went up the hill	12
Jack be nimble, Jack be quick	38
Ladybug, ladybug, fly away home	40
Little Jack Horner	22
Little Miss Muffet	30
Mary had a little lamb	32
Mary, Mary, quite contrary	28
Oh, the grand old Duke of York	26
Old King Cole was a merry old soul	10
Oranges and lemons	14
Rain, rain, go away	4
Ring-a-ring o' roses	16
Rock-a-bye, baby, on the treetop	42
Seesaw, Margery Daw	34
Sing a song of sixpence	18
Thirty days hath September	8

FROM THE AUTHOR

 I have always been fascinated by mysteries. So for me, nursery rhymes and stories labeled "traditional" or written by a shadowy figure called "anonymous" have always been mysteries waiting to be solved.

In fact, writing this book was like writing a detective story. There I was, like Sherlock Holmes, hot on the trail for clues and likely suspects: "All right, Mother Goose, we want the *real* story about Humpty Dumpty and Little Jack Horner. And while you're at it, give us the "skinny" on all these oranges and lemons, and what about this Jack and Jill who went up the hill?" This book is what I found out.

Who Knows?

The Midnight Pig
PS I Love You, Gramps
Humphrey
Dinosaur Girl

The Dinosaur Connection
Myth or Mystery?
Hairy Little Critters
A Pocket Full of Posies

Written by **Alan Trussell-Cullen**
Illustrated by **Marie Low, Ian McNee, Philip Webb, Bryan Pollard,** and **Lyn Kriegler**

© 1999 Shortland Publications Inc.
All rights reserved. No part of this publication may be reproduced or transmitted in any form or by any means, electronic or mechanical, including photocopying, recording, taping, or any information storage and retrieval system, without permission in writing from the publisher.

05 04 03 02 01 00 99
10 9 8 7 6 5 4 3 2 1

Published in the United States by

a division of Reed Elsevier Inc.
500 Coventry Lane
Crystal Lake, IL 60014

Printed in Hong Kong
ISBN: 0-7901-1836-X